TREASURES
THROUGH AN
OPENING DOOR

VALERIE EDWARDS

BALBOA.PRESS
A DIVISION OF HAY HOUSE

Balboa Press books may be ordered through booksellers or by contacting:

Balboa Press
A Division of Hay House
1663 Liberty Drive
Bloomington, IN 47403
www.balboapress.com.au
AU TFN: 1 800 844 925 (Toll Free inside Australia)
AU Local: 0283 107 086 (+61 2 8310 7086 from outside Australia)

Print information available on the last page.

ISBN: 978-1-5043-2332-1 (sc)
ISBN: 978-1-5043-2333-8 (e)

Balboa Press rev. date: 11/09/2020

CONTENTS

COVERS

What does it matter
The way that we look?
For we are just a cover
The same as on any book
Does the cover reveal
The contents inside
Or is it just an image
Behind which we hide
Do we look to the cover
To find the truth
Of the chapter we are reading
Inside the book
Or is the cover merely just that
A cover to protect
Keep the story safe
From the rough handling
It sometimes receives
The dust it collects
When it just sits
Not daring to open
To reveal to the world
What resides inside
Behind the cover
Inside each page
A story unfolds
Or is it a play
Are we afraid to accept
The starring role?

Behind others
Do we wish to go
Follow in their footsteps
Never making our own
For fear of failure
Looking a fool
What others think
Matters more to you
Then the expressions
Bottled up inside
Never given the chance
To find out
What they could do
Hiding behind a cover
That is ever changing

THE WIND ON THE SEA

The wind is in a playful mood
She skips across the sea
Creating little ripples
On waters deep and green

The wind is in a restless mood
She can't make up her mind
She huffs and puffs
From all compass points
Direction hard to find

The wind is feeling irritable
Blowing hot and cold
Stirring up the ocean
Watching the waves roll

The wind is in a temper
She sends waves crashing to the shore
White horses ride the ocean swell
I hear their mighty roar

The wind is now serine
The sea so still and flat
Fish the only ripples make
I feel nothing on my back

GARDEN OF PLENTY

In the garden of plenty I stand alone
Lifeless and thorny on my own
I hide in a corner beside beautiful flowers
Bright green shrubs and tuberose
Vines with perfume sickly sweet
Climb over the fence and into the creek
But here I stand year after year
With a collection of dead wood hiding me
Inside I feel retched misunderstood
Powerless to free myself of the dead wood
That holds me back weighs me down
Keeps my roots from breaking new ground
Spreading and seeking discovering anew
One day a new gardener arrives on the scene
I shake in my boots as he stands over me
Will he rip me from the Earth or prune me free
Cut back the dead wood strip me bare
To stand naked exposed nowhere to hide
From my neighbours prying eyes
He goes to his barrow chooses a tool
With a pruning knife in his hand
He sets to work strips me down
He clips and snips stands back to admire
The naked stem before his eyes
He takes a step back smiles and says
You'll do fine with a little water and
Poo from the cows behind
To my neighbours I know I am just a stick

No glossy leaves or beautiful flowers
Adorn my trunk hour after hour
But, in a while you will see
Just how God imagined me
With all the dead wood cut away
Come the spring
I will amaze

CONNECTION

When the door is open and the light shines through
A new Soul emerges to connect with you
He is patient and calm willing to wait
For eons if he must until your wide awake
He will stay in the shadows come when you call
Retreat once again when your interest stalls
It may take lifetimes or the blink of an eye
But desert you he won't
He will stay by your side

HEAVY OF HEART

My heart grows heavy
With each passing day
As I watch your life slip away
I know not the hour or the day
That you will leave pass away
To a place I cannot see
I will be alone with my tears
I must be strong happy gay
Enjoy each moment of the day
Have no regrets guilt or fear
A better place waits for thee
Where I will follow
At some point in time
And life once again
Will be sublime

AGE

Some find age a burden
They grumble through their lives
They lock themselves behind closed doors
The sun they never find

Some find age a pleasure
They sleep until noon or more
Then they rise switch the TV on
Never opening their door

Some find age an adventure
Where at last, they are free to roam
They get up with the sparrows
And head out to explore

Some find age a blessing
They meditate and sow
Seeds that bring great happiness
To everyone they know

Age is like a Ferris-wheel
It starts off very slow
Then gathers its momentum
With every year that goes
So do not take life for granted
Cherish every day
Smile and let the sunshine in
Say what a beautiful day

INNER PEACE

Inner peace is what we crave
An elusive thought that slips away
It is in our grasp time after time
Then someone says something unkind
We fall back for it plays on our mind
It can be something simple
That was said without thought
However, it can bring us down and destroy
We must be strong and brush it aside
Dwell on it not and it will subside
Learn to turn the other cheek
For this world, don't you know?
Belongs to the meek

AGELESS BEING

The pathway narrows out
With every step we take
Where once we would have stumbled
We now stand tall and straight
For we have inner vision
That enables us to see
All the many potholes
Placed in front of thee
The branches are less often
Shall I turn left or right
But now we know the middle
Is the one that sheds the light
Some see age with terror
Some see age with pride
Some see age with wisdom
Knowing true beauty is inside
We all have a shadow
A dark side some may say
That we must face to conquer
Fears we meet along the way
With every fear we conquer
With every fear we face
The shadow grows much dimmer
As light steps in its place
I know you have the courage
I know you have the strength
To fill your being with sunlight
That shadows can't hide in

For you have travelled many paths
Rested here and there
Not always choosing the easy path
For what would you find there
Not the buried treasure
We sometimes stumble on
When we choose the steeper path
That fewer travel on
Trust your intuition
The voice you hear inside
When others stand in your way
Ask them to step aside
Knowing in your journey
That you must stand alone
When your journey is over
And your maker calls you home

FACES

I sometimes look with wonder at the faces all around
I wonder at the sorrow and pain that can be found
Etched in the faces of people that I meet
Of people sharing air space in buses trains and planes
Who hurry about their business with no time for a chat
With no time to be happy to rejoice in whom they are
We all know love is a wonderful thing
It can make us weep
It can make our heart sing
It can take us to the depths of despair
It can lift us so high we don't have a care
But once love has touched you and set you aflame
You know you will never be the same
Your heart feels elation your soul wants to soar
It is as if you have opened an invisible door
Where emotions are heightened feelings released
When we open our heart to love
Whether it be for ourselves or someone else
It transforms our lives in so many ways
Nothing will ever be quite the same
It is an inner strength that sets us apart
This feeling of love welling up from the heart
Though we cannot define it, we know it is there
For it makes us forget our woes and cares
Love can grow stronger flow with the tide
Of mixed emotions that we feel inside
If we nourish love daily set time aside

Never hiding mixed emotions welling up inside
For if we ignore them store them away
They will grow and fester
Love will decay

DREAMS

Life is full of hopes and dreams
Dreams of health dreams of wealth
Dreams of success and what else
Dreams of a future with someone who cares
Of someone to love and someone to share
Someone to cherish when we get old
Dreams of a better place to live
Where we have much to share and give
To help someone along the way
To share the laughter and the tears

DREAMING

I love to sit and daydream
To go to distant lands
To frolic in the forests
To walk across the sands
To travel to the mountaintops where I can sit and gaze
Out to other galaxies that set the sky ablaze
The stars that twinkle in the sky look down on Mother Earth
They see she has lost her sparkle
They know that she is cursed
There are so many planets in the universe
And there are a few just the same as Earth
With people who are thoughtless and have lost their way
They only think of living just from day to day
They have no thought for the future
Of the actions that they take
For future generations
Who must live in their wake
They go about their busines
Consumed by their greed
Knowing they are destroying
Their subconscious
They will not heed
They find many excuses
For the actions that they take
They turn it all around
Hero's, of themselves they do make
Others are overawed
By their power and their wealth

They turn their heads away
Hide the truth from themselves
They like the many comforts
The results of their greed
Who gives a damn
About killing a few trees
Oil spills in the oceans
Rockets in the sky
Nuclear reactors
Are a necessity
The minerals we are taking
Mother Earth does not need
The creeks that are poisoned
By the factories
The list is endless
It grows longer day-by-day
But just how long can
The Earth go on this way
Before she retaliates
Can no longer stand the pain
She will roll in her fury
On her axis she will turn
The results of their actions
Man, at last must discern

DOUBT

When doubt fills voids
Inside your mind
Do not feel pressured
Try to unwind
Go for a walk
Bide your time
Let your thoughts wonder
FANTASIZE
Cleanse your mind
Of worry of fear
With each out breath
Set your mind free
Release the tensions
That paralyse
Breathe – breathe – breathe
Until all thoughts
Subside
Then once the mind
Is calm and clear
Tune into your body
What do you feel
Trust your instincts
Over your mind
Truth comes from within
Time after time

TREES, TREES, BEAUTIFUL TREES

Trees, trees, beautiful trees
They make all the air we breathe
They give us shade they cool the Earth
They are creatures of the universe
They have been here since day one
Making a place for us in the sun
They come in many shapes and forms
Some give us food some keep us warm
Some give us shade from the blazing sun
To sit and relax when work is done
Some give us colour in many shades
Flowers to take your breath away
Some die back when winter comes
So as not to keep us from the sun
So, we can warm our weary bones
Then they grow back when summer returns
Their aim is to please to live as one
For they are Gods favourite son

He gave them to us to love and adore
But we never even saw
That they have feelings just like the rest
That we should treat them with respect
For without them we could not survive
To watch another beautiful sunrise

GRANDMOTHER MOON

The moon shines down on slumber land
Her beams spreading far and wide
Lighting the way for travellers
Who travel throughout the night
As we sleep, she ebbs and flows
Pulling us to and throw
Whispering the answers
To all we want to know
For she is full of wisdom
Looking down from up above
All the waters in the oceans
Heed her beck and call

A CARER'S WORLD

I sit and ponder who I am
What is my place in this foreign land
Am I the parent, the adult, the child
Please help me God for I have lost control
Of this life that was once simple and free
I feel panic building inside of me
Doctors and nurses, blood tests and screens
What, dear God does it all mean
I need a degree to wade through the pile
Of brochures, and leaflets and internet scrolls
I sit by his bedside day after day
Searching my mind for something to say
Should I be chirpy
Should I be gay
Should I say to my love it's a beautiful day
The sun is shining
The sky is blue
But when I look into his eyes
None of this is true
Our world is in turmoil
Our future unsure
Storm clouds have gathered outside our door
Will they blow over
Turn into a squall
Will my tears fall like raindrops
Will the grim reaper call
I know not the answers
I walk the unknown

Path to the future that beckons me on
I live for each moment
Keep my hopes high
Behind every storm cloud
A rainbow in the sky

MARTIN'S POEM

I have a very special friend
Who was mine for a little while
To love to feed to comfort
And to watch him grow
Then I had to set him free
To find his very soul
It is a path that is not easy
There are many twists and turns
So much, we must experience
So much, we have to learn
It is filled with many hurdles
Some so hard to cross
And at the time we feel
So very, very lost
Our heart grows heavy
We know not which way to turn
The hills turn into mountains
With every twist and turn
Then a pathway opens
A door springs into sight
A door that slowly opens
We begin to see the light
As we slowly enter
It really becomes quite clear
The path we have been taking
Was meant to lead us here
Then our world starts changing
We are consumed with love

The heart that was so heavy
Has lightened up with love
We feel that life has meaning
We know we are here to learn
Now we do look forward
To the many twists and turns
For we know we are growing
When we open up the door
Let the light come streaming in
Now our soul can really soar
Not confined to bodies
That are just an empty shell
With all the doors shut up tight
In darkness they must dwell
But now the door has opened
The light is shining through
Now your heart is filled with love
Just like the love I feel for you

THE CALL OF DEATH

Death comes to all
Be it the still of the night
A clear summers day
Spring winter or fall
But be not afraid
When Death comes knocking
Calling your name
Her breath is sweet
Like summer rain
Her smile is gentle
Her thoughts are kind
She has your best interest
On her mind
So be not afraid
When you hear Deaths call
She is welcoming you home
Back into the fold
For life is but a moment in time
A grand illusion
To stretch your mind
To create to explore
To love to endue
To raise your vibrations
So, your Soul can soar
Lift the veil that covers your eyes
Let your senses overshadow your mind
When Death calls and your Earthly life ends
Your Soul floats free

A new adventure begins
So do not fool yourself
Thinking Death is the end
For you come back to Earth
Again, and again
New body new name
New point of view
It is a beautiful time
When Death comes for you

FOR MOTHER'S EVERYWHERE

Mothers are special
They help us to grow
To develop our nature
So that we may show
Our strengths and our weakness
Our joy and pain
But love ourselves
Just the same
For she does not judge us
Or set us aside
For the love in her heart
Can never die
It is buried so deep
As she waves us goodbye
Her children may wander
Scatter afar
But her love reaches out
With invisible arms
Over mountains and valleys
Oceans and planes
To gather us up
Dry our tears
Pat our backs
Console our fears
Now mother I would like

To tell you this day
How wonderful you are
In every way
I love you mum

THE INDIAN WAY

The Indian brave and his squaw
Had something special
They both adored
Looking at the stars at night
It filled them with wonder and delight
They would wander hand in hand
Talk about the Promised Land
With Mother Nature they would converse
They would talk about the universe
About the moon and the sun
How the Earth first begun
They would speak to the Eagle and the Crow
Of the magic that made things grow
They would call to the wind
They knew him by name
Ask him to bring in the rain
To fill the rivers and the creeks
So, there would be plenty of water to drink
They would stay in one place for only a while
Then they would move so as not to spoil
With Mother Nature they were so in tune
They could tell the days by the moon
They knew the herbs that nature supplied
Which ones to eat which ones to dry
To save for the future in times of need
They had a witch doctor who spoke to the Gods
He would always get the nod
Of approval for future events

Everyone was so content
The sound of laughter would fill the air
When in the evening they all shared
They sat around the huge campfire
And stories they would tell
To keep alive
The things they had experienced
In days gone by
They had no need for paper or pen
To cut down a tree was forbidden
They would clean up all the old dead wood
To use in their fires as they should
When it was gone, they would look around
To leave no trace
To leave just as they had found
For they knew they would again return
When nature had supplies once more
They would sometimes walk through the night
The children would ride with the old woman
On ponies who were their friends
Until they came once more to the chosen place
That nature supplied for this gentle race
They were a special breed of men
On which Mother Nature knew she could depend
They would treat all creatures with respect
Then they would only select
What they needed to feed the clan
Never let the killing get out of hand
They thanked the Gods for what they received
Prayed they left no one to grieve
They tried to take the old and weak
Whose time had come for they could not compete
This is the way that we must go
This is the future that we must sow

With Mother Nature we must not compete
For she has grown so very weak
We must build her resources day by day
Then in the future, she will gladly repay
With an abundance of supplies
That we will hardly believe our eyes
All her creatures we must treat with respect
We must never, never forget
That all these creatures are really our friends
That we all from heaven do descend

IMPOSSIBLE DREAM

I love to see colour everywhere
I love to see colour and breathe fresh clean air
I love to gaze at the stars on a clear summer night
To gaze at the stars fills me with wonder and delight
To walk through the forest in the drizzling rain
Fills me with hope once again
Hope for the future to learn from the past
Not to cause anymore-nuclear blasts
To treat the Earth with love and respect
Not to ignore and neglect
To take for granted the wealth that she shares
To go right on taking when we are stripping her bare
We must realise that she feels pain
To just keep on taking is insane
We must replenish with love and care
Give her time to rest and repair
The damage we have caused through years of neglect
Of taking not giving in every respect
Of poisoning the air and the soil
Of stripping her naked of all her reserves
Now we must wait give her time to repair
Treat her with love, plant trees everywhere
Grow back the forests that have been destroyed
Clean up the oceans, the rivers, the streams
You know we can do it
It is not an Impossible Dream
We must work together we cannot do it apart
Hope eternal must spring from the heart

THINK AS ONE

The wheel is turning a little faster each day
It is time to get down on our knees and pray
For peace and harmony here on Earth
To go back in time and mend the curse
To heal the destruction
To ease the pain
To once more reach and reclaim
The right to rule with gentle hand
To rule with love that we all understand
In tune with nature in tune with the Earth
With the Sun Moon Stars and the Universe
It is time not for pity
But for strength and love
For all to unite
Think as one

THE SILVER THREAD

An arrow has fallen
It has landed somewhere
Out of sight of those who care
It is an arrow of peace and love
Of wisdom and joy from those above
The arrow is wooden with no bow attached
Just a silver thread woven with love
This thread is endless
It goes on and on
From dimension to dimension
With grace and love
I feel its power its strength divine
This silver thread is yours and mine
It is our connection our safety line
Now we can struggle to set ourselves free
From the strings that bind us to eternity
They may all break and fall away
But the silver thread is here to stay
The further you fall the longer the climb
Up the silver thread of time
It is woven with love stronger than steel
This silver thread that is connected to you
When death steps in darkens your door
Your silver thread transforms once more
A tunnel of light that beckons you in
To walk through the pearly gates again
To enter the light to forget your fear
To look for your loved ones gathering near

To welcome you home back into the fold
For your safety line will always hold
You may at times stumble lose your way
Get lost in the smog of Earths decay
You may be weak when temptation calls
And easy money is at your door
Or it may be lust greed or pride
That brings you down makes you slide
Do not give up or be filled with despair
If you are on a downer or lost somewhere
Do not call yourself weak a blithering fool
I am sure these steps were laid out for you
A path to follow to experience and grow
Just some wild oats you needed to sow
If we do not, experience we never know
How someone else is suffering so
We cannot feel their pain wipe away their tears
We cannot explain how they must face their fears
If we do not have the wisdom that experience brings
We cannot be judgmental if we already know
Deep in our hearts, they are seeds we have sown
Mistakes we have made maybe lifetimes gone by
Search deep in our hearts to the depth of our soul
That lifetime may feel just a moment ago
So do not look down or turn your head away
Stretch out your hand give a smile instead
Do not feel you will be tainted, filled with appal
The experience will enrich your soul
If you do this with love, only love will survive
Lift you up through the silver thread of time
Up through dimensions your vibrations will rise
When empathy is your guide
A pillar of strength a monument of steel
You will become for the golden rule

Do unto others, as you would have them do unto you
If you live by this rule and live in the now
Moment by moment of each precious hour
Your life will transform in a miraculous way
For you will at last have found the way

CREATION

God made many creatures and he loves them all
Be they very large or be they very small
Whether they're in the oceans
Or on the mountain plains
It gives him great pleasure
To watch them at their games
He made man in his image
Gave him a will of his own
To make his own decisions
To sit upon his throne
To rule with Mother Nature
To lend a helping hand
To cherish all God's creatures
Help things go to plan
But things went very wrong
Man got out of hand
He found that he liked power
To be in control
Over all God's creatures
He really lost his soul
He became full of greed
Not caring who he hurt
Or who he deceived
The world was his oyster
He felt that he was grand
He forgot all about
Giving a helping hand
He sought to destroy

What he could not control
He killed just for greed
For money and for fun
He couldn't see the pain
Or the injustice he had done
He thought it very funny
As they died in pain
Or called out to their mother's
But it was all in vain
For his heart was hardened
He could not hear their cries
All he could see was the dollar signs
He hunted to extinction
He did not give a damn
Now God in heaven is filled with despair
At all the suffering man is causing here
He gave him free will a mind of his own
So, he could live in comfort
Reap what he had sown
But man has sown destruction
In the skies the sea the air
He killed all God's creatures
He does not even care
That Mother Earth is dying
She is down on her knees
Begging for help
For she cannot breathe
We must go back to basics
Get rid of greed
Cherish all God's creatures
Help Mother Earth breathe
Clean up the oceans plant more trees
Clean the skies the universe
The very air we breathe

LET NATURE BE YOUR GUIDE

I like the feel of wind in my hair
Rain upon my skin
Sunshine and laughter go hand in hand
With running along a beach
A mountain stream
A forest tall
Soft grass beneath my feet
You can't beat a day spent in nature
To make one's life complete
For nature brings one close to God
An elation of the Soul
A rise in one's vibrations
When natures in control
So, take the time to seek her out
Make her a part of your life
You will reap the benefits
Of a happier healthier life

TIS THE LITTLE THINGS

My heart is heavy I feel so alone
On a distant shore far from home
I have lived
I've loved
I've laughed
I've cried
I've told the truth
Sometimes I've lied
Tis the little things in life
It's true
That brings us hope
For life anew
Things that grow
That breathe, that feel
That fill our senses
That make us real
Lift us up
From the depths of despair
Rejuvenate and repair
Make us whole
Reconnect our Soul

DEATH CANNOT PART US

The time has come for us to part
But you will always live in my heart
With every beat I feel you near
I hear your voice crystal clear
Death cannot part us
Our connection is strong
Over eons of lifetimes
Our love remains true
So goodbye my love
Until we meet again
On this Earth or another plane
I blow you kisses
Call softly your name
Carried by the wind
For you to claim

TREES

A tree can be such an awesome sight
We look with wonder and delight
At the frame of these gentle giants
Who reach, out to the Universe
Who give, us shade to cool the Earth
Where on a long hot summer's day
We can sit to read or play
Trees even shape the air we breathe
They give so much
But what, do they receive
The cold hard steel of the axe man's blade
A poison drink, a copper nail
The serrated edge of a saw
Bulldozers with chains that brutalise
Leaving, the forest a desecrated land
Where not even a shrub can stand
A barren waste where no rain falls
A twofold blade to the sword
The world sits back not raising a hand
The trees suffer in silence
So does the land
The animals that lived within the walls
Have been forgotten, no one hears their calls
The Earth is dying splitting apart
Her silent voice asking
Do you, have no heart
Do you, not see the destruction
Hear the cries

Of these gentle giants
Who have, no way to stand and fight
The many, many invisible men
Whose greed, power, wealth and toil
Are stealing the treasures that belong to us all
Wake up from your slumber
Become more aware
Don't say you don't know
Or worse - you don't care
One voice is a whisper
Added to many a roar
Like a drop in the ocean
It will reach every shore
Put an end to the curse
Of greedy inconsiderate man
So that peace on Earth
May reign again

Trees are special can you not see
We need them all so we can breathe
Drink pure water eat fresh food
Leave a future for our children
And their children too

A LOVE POEM

A poem of love I have found
One that makes the world go around
Love is a feeling that we share
With someone special you cannot compare
With any other living soul
And with whom you desire to grow old
You want them in your bed at night
That you may touch and delight
You want to share your hopes, your dreams
You're innermost secrets and your fears
You want to build a home for two
Fill it with love in every room
To fill it with laughter and with fun
Where you both come when your day is done
Then one day you may have a special surprise
That will light up your faces and your eyes
A gift from God a little soul
For you to cherish and behold
Your love will grow stronger it will expand
There will be no more time for holding hands
Your days will be filled with nappies and toys
Your nights with the cries of a hungry new born
But things will settle down once more
Give you time to enjoy
The family that you both have made
Plan what you will do in your old age

The years fly by the kids have grown
Soon you will find you are both alone
Alone as it was at the start
When love first bloomed in your heart

CREATURES FROM THE SEA

The sea is really a wondrous place
Too beautiful to ignore
It holds many dangers and much to explore
There are so many creatures
Who live, beneath the sea
To enter in these waters
You must be very brave
But if you find the courage
To go down and explore
You will be amazed
At what she holds in store
All the colours of the rainbow
In different shapes and size
Some with bodies that change
Before your very eyes
They swim amidst their garden
That sways with the tide
Some of them play hide and seek
Some of them must die
As food for another of a different kind
But they do not kill for pleasure
Or just for fun
They kill to keep the numbers down
For food on the run
They all live in harmony
Side by side
Some live on others backs
Some go for a ride

It is a world of wonder
Down below the waves
That you can discover
If you are very brave
But please do remember
Before you take the plunge
That these are all God's creatures
Do not kill just for fun

THE JOURNEY

I caught a train to central
Sat back and watched the view
A countryside ever changing
Came sliding into view
The station stops were many
The people crowed in
All with destinations know only to them
I see a plane about to land
Emerge from a clouded sky
I wonder about the people
Why they chose to fly
There are many forms of travel
Many ways to fly
Many destinations
Some that make us cry
For we all are on a journey
Although we may not know
The travel stops are many
The transport sometimes slow
At times we get so weary
Wonder what is to be gained
By staying with this journey
When we would rather jump off the plane
Still we keep on traveling
Though we know not why
Maybe something special
Is waiting at the end of the ride
Hope must spring eternal

When we purchase a ticket to ride
Have faith that the engine driver
Is always on your side
Although you cannot see him
Try as hard as you might
His presence is ever constant
On this wondrous flight
Know you have the power
As hard as it may seem
To change your destination
Is not an impossible dream

COLOURS

All the colours of the rainbow
You are encased within
Some of them go on and off
Depending on the mood you are in
Pink is for pleasure
For all your hopes and dreams
Purple tells us that all is not quite as it seems
Yellow is for sunshine where happy thoughts abound
Blue is for curing all ill that is to be found
Green is for learning, learning something new
In just the way that I am teaching this to you
White is for purity where pure thoughts are found
Red is for anger or when danger is around
Orange is quite special
It is better than the rest
And when this lesson is over
I will put you to the test
For orange means it is working
The things that you have learned
And orange is the colour of the first new born thought
That springs to mind when the lesson is learnt
Now look very carefully at the people you meet
Or even at the people walking down the street
For the colour of the rainbow
Shining around their head
Go out and practice now this lessons' through
Maybe very soon you will see the colours too

NIGHT SKY

I look at the night sky
What, do I see
Sparkling eyes
Looking down on me
Stirring my senses
Penetrating my brain
A feeling so awesome
I find it hard to explain
My heart it beats faster
My eyes start to tear
My thoughts are in turmoil
I long to be free
To soar through the heavens
Streak past the stars
A body-less being
Free at last

THE COLOUR GOLD

Gold is the colour of the Universe
Gold sets us apart from the Earth
For when we see gold all around
We know it is for real
A channel we have found
A channel with an open mind
Who, is full of love for human kind
Who would be willing to light the path
For others to follow and find their way
They do not mind being different
They do not follow like sheep
This does not mean
They are not mild and meek
It just means they are stronger
That they can stand-alone
They do not rely on others
They have a mind of their own
They go with what they feel inside
They realise they have nothing to hide
They do not stand and preach at the garden gate
But are open to others who will seek them out
For they radiate a special charm
Others can see that they mean no harm
Some time, in the future that is not far away
They will teach everyone from near and far
Teach how to heal with power and love
With power that is sent from the Lord above

But the power will not go to their head
For they are meeker and milder than all the rest
Look to the future forget the past
For your moment in time is approaching fast

THE COLOUR GREEN

Green is a colour that is seen everywhere
Green is like a breath of fresh air
Green exhilarates
Green calms us down
Green is where nature is to be found
Mother Earth wears green as a crown
Green in our aura means success
Green means we have past every test
That Earth can offer in this point in time
Now we are out to pasture
Just filling in time
Green is also a powerful tool
If we use it with love
And do not play the fool
Green has the power the power to heal
All our ills if we only knew
To heal the sick with grace and love
If we draw on the strength from the one above
Every colour has a use
If we use it with love and not abuse

THOUGHTS

A thought is something we try to express
To tell the world about our success
About the things that we have planned
Or about how we are going to make a stand
We all have thoughts that we want to share
Plans to make with someone who cares
Thoughts about the Universe
Why, oh why was Mother Earth cursed
We all make decisions that we sometimes regret
We neglect to notice others mistakes
Open our eyes when it is almost too late
Or we just can't be bothered we let things go
Hoping someone else will notice and say no
They will take a stand and put to an end
When all we want to do is pretend
That we do not notice we don't really care
It is none of our business to interfere
If we just wait it will all go away
But this mess will end up in our lap one day
We are all responsible we must make a stand
Give the environment a helping hand
With Mother Nature we all must work
And her treasures with us she will share
If we all really care, we must care
Help make decisions about Our Earth
And what we are doing to the universe

MOTHER LOVE

A mother loves her children with a special love
It cannot be explained it comes down from above
In such abundance there are no words to speak
That can describe it would take a week
Of searching through the volumes of books we have
That give a word its meaning
And then we would feel so sad
For there are no words to describe
The feeling that she has
Look no more my children for that special word
That fills the hearts of mothers in all parts of the world
As mothers love their children you should love the World
For it is something special a gift from God above
Something we should treasure with a mother's love

CHILDREN

Children are very special
Their love never dies
It keeps on growing stronger as the years go by
They put aside their pleasure to lend a helping hand
They never grumble when things do not go to plan
They give love new meaning it comes straight from the heart
They always keep their head when others fights do start
They remember all the many things
mother did when they were small
They cherish all the memories and love to recall
The years they spent together when times were tough
And mother gave so very much without any fuss
Now the roles reversed and mothers very small
And they come a running all she has to do is call
It gives them great pleasure
It comes straight from the heart
They will never, never, let the teardrops start
For life is much too precious to let things get in the way
It gives life new meaning every time they say
The word that gives so much pleasure
To mothers around the world
To simply say I love you
And mean every word

SUMMER RAIN

Summer rain will sometimes fall
We hardly notice it at all
It comes in the evening when the work is done
So as not to spoil our summer fun
It comes down in buckets
Its smell fills the air
It flows through the gutters and we do not care
That it is wasted goes out to sea
To mix with the salt become just a memory
When we could have saved it if we only had tried
To use in our gardens and have excess supplies
Now we will suffer when the rains cease
Moan to our friends that there is no release
From the restrictions that the council impose
When all we had to do was hook up a hose
To the connection nature supplies
Then we would have water up to our eyes

LETS

Let us lift the many shadows that form before our eyes
That we may have clear vision and see beyond the skies
Let us whisk away the darkness so there is only light
That we may travel safely on our rise to greater heights
Let us fill our heart with sunshine so it may overflow
Gladden the hearts of others we meet wherever we go
Let us fill our words with meaning so love and truth may flow
Into the lives of the many children that we know
Let us teach them about laughter for laughter heals the soul
And who can find fear and hate where joy just overflows

SUMMERLAND

My little one can you not see
As I am part of you, you are part of me
It is so simple if you only knew
I am the memory deep within you
I am the spark that flickers inside
Lighting your way, I act as your guide
Planting the seeds of thought in your mind
I have been waiting a long, long time
Waiting for you to awaken and know
I am the one who loves you so
I am the part you set aside
When you volunteered for life this time
We have lived so many lives
Sometimes apart, sometimes side by side
Sometimes we merge into one
I am the anchor I hold the key
To all the parts you cannot see
Soon we will merge once more into one
For the moment will have come
To set into action the course that we planned
When we were in the Summerland

THE GROWING LIST

The sound of distant thunder is ringing in my ears
It makes me want to hide and too conceal my fears
My fears for the future, my fears for the Earth
For future generations for the creatures of this World
Will they ever manage to undo what we have done
To feed the growing numbers of hungry on the run
These are the displaced people
Whose country have turned away
Threatened to destroy if they would not obey

The children of these Nations are so sick inside
They do not wish to live yet they do not wish to die
They have no faith in the future they have no place to go
They feel so unclean and oh so all alone
They have become just a number on a growing list
That people choose to deny pretend do not exist
They die by the roadside become food for the crows
But they are not a feast for they were only skin and bone
And who will remember who is left to mourn
Insignificant little souls whose lives have been cut so short

NO TIME TO WASTE

I open my eyes but cannot see
The beauty of all that surrounds me
The birds the trees the sky so blue
The grass so green the flowers too
For I am so busy I have no time
The clock is ticking the hours fly by
Appointments to keep drinks at the bar
Then off to the gym I must work hard
I must work at the weekend
Put in extra hours so I can buy my new car
A house a boat a caravan too
Then I will be happy I will not sing the blues
Once the shine wears off our many new toys
We will seek out new items to bring us joy
It's an unending cycle a merry go round
Of highs and lows ups and downs
Stop for a moment open your eyes
Breath in the beauty nature supplies
Take in the mountains the oceans the streams
Understand that joy comes from within

FAITH

We must have faith if we are to grow
Faith in what we feel in both our heart and soul
Faith can move mountains wipe out pain
Pick up the pieces let us start again
Faith must stand firm when doubt rushes in
Filling our mind clouding our thoughts
Breaking our heart with unkind words
When doubt rushes in darkens your mind
Turn to your faith time after time
Pray for help protection and strength
Believe that you can pass this test
Believe in the wonderful soul that you are
That you can be seen from afar
Believe that you are not alone
That you are never far from home
Believe in your weakness and your strength
A total you who can let down their defence
Can be open and honest carefree and gay
If you live in the now there is no other way
Faith opens the mind frees the soul
Makes you complete lets you be whole
Faith can take on many shapes and forms
It can gladden your heart make you warm
It can come in a package of sorrow and pain
When you feel, you are lost with nothing to gain
Faith can be seen in the eyes of a child
Whose innocence has left them whole
No thought of fear darkens their mind

Hems them in time after time
Faith can also be seen in the eyes of the old Buda
Who has cast aside all possessions
Greed and pride
Let faith enter be your guide
Trust that faith is on your side
Be open and honest loving and free
Faith will do the rest for thee

THE SPARROW

A sparrow has fallen from the sky
It landed on the Earth without a cry
It felt no sorrow, nor no pain
Its body was shaken its soul was torn free
To fly with the Eagles the Golden Goose
To merge with the raindrops the stars in the sky
Now the little sparrow really can fly
Its wingspan has widened its power increased
It is no longer a detestable little beast
It is a great Eagle, A Hawk. A Dove of Peace

SET THEM FREE

As it was in the beginning
It will be in the end
Ashes to ashes
Dust to dust
A return to the element
Is a must
For as we travel
Through space and time
A cumbersome body
Would cloud the mind
Hem us in slow us down
Connect us to Earth
When we are Heaven bound
Do not mourn
When loved ones pass through
They leave their body
As a reminder to you
That you may remember
The good times you shared
The love the tears
The joy the fears
The challenges you faced
Along the way
Are nothing to the one
You face today
Just remember
When you lay them down
To a soft spot in the ground

Or toss their ashes
Into the sea
That this is just a body
Do not mourn for thee
For as the body
Must now turn to dust
The soul soars free
To merge with the wind
An invisible force
Spreading their wings
Blowing you kisses
Drying your eyes
Begging you please
Not to cry
Be happy rejoice
Set them free
To continue their journey
Of discovery

CHANGE

What is this feeling I cannot ignore
It unsettles me on a distant shore
I know not the answers
I need time to explore
The inner voice I sense within
The World has changed
From the World I once knew
Different ideas
Different points of view
Where do I fit
In this strange new land
Do I simply bury my head in the sand
Pretend I don't notice
Try to fit in
Although I don't like it
Not one little bit
Follow the rules
Mindless people have set
Pitting Nation against Nation
To cover the mess
They have created
And oh! What a mess
Wars and famine
Disease caused by greed
The killing of creatures
When there is no need
Deforesting lands
To make a quick buck

Wanton destruction
Across the globe
Where will it end
Nobody knows
Warnings we are given
But who takes heed
The minority of man
Who no one believes
Nature is tiring
Of our vandalistic ways
The time is coming
When we must pay
When we must reap
What we have sown
It is the innocent folk
Who must carry the load
Face the wrath
Of Nature and Nations
Wake up wake up
Before it's too late
Rise with one voice
And say
No!
To senseless wars
To senseless killing
To starving children
In the millions

THE SWEETEST MYSTERY

I used to think that life was tough
A mountain hard to climb
With pot holes large as craters
Waiting there for me to find

I used to think that life was hard
Money in short supply
I never counted the blessings
That money cannot buy

Now that I am older
And time is running out
The things that money cannot buy
I cannot do without

I treasure every rainbow
Each bird that flutters by
The sound of its voice
So rich
Brings tears to my eyes

The sky at night a wonder
It sparkles like a jewel
With shooting stars and satellites
Streaking past the moon

The things that mother nature
Hands out for free
Now fill me with the awe of life
The sweetest mystery

SIMPLICITY

The rule is simple
You cannot go wrong
Guide your thoughts
Do not muddle along
Keep your mind clear
Your heart filled with love
Create and environment
To be proud of
Let beauty surround you
Wherever you be
Close your eyes to horror
Set yourself free
Think only of sunshine
When doubt gathers around
Do not let sorrow befall you
Drag you down
The Worlds full of wonder
If only you knew
The sky is the limit
When you believe this to be true

LETTING GO

What do you say
To smooth the way
To erase the fear
The remorse the tears
How can you relay
Pave the way
To a transition that is tranquil
A mind free of doubt
A heart full of joy
To be free at last
Free of a body that weighs you down
Anchors you to Earth
When your Soul longs to soar
To other dimensions
Where loved ones wait
To guide you home
To recuperate

LOOK AT ME

Look at me I am free to fly
To any dimension in the sky
I do not need an anchor to weigh me down
Keep my head buried in the sand
No need for guilt sorrow or pain
No ego trip down memory lane
I am free to travel my soul can soar
I now can open another door

THE MAGIC WORD

Why do we laugh when we should cry
Why do we wait until things die to say
I love you
For this is the thing that we should say
It works its magic every day
We say it
Open your hearts ease your minds
It will be much easier you will find
With practice
For love is a word that tells a lot
About how we feel but cannot express
It is magic
Love is a wondrous thing you know
It is what we feel with our heart and soul
Nothing else can match it
For it helps us understand
Something of what God has planned
If we would only trust him
In the future you will see
Love is but a memory
If we only knew it
Trust this love that you feel
Always remember
The golden rule
You were given
For if you live by this rule
And practice what you know is true
All else will be forgiven

Open up your hearts and minds
If you would only try to find
This love for one another
There would be no more need
For greed war or famine

THE DRUM BEAT

The drum beats in the heart of man
It has been there since time began
The softer the drum the louder the call
Harkin to it one and all
Dance to your tune the sound of your drum
Make your sound number one
The top of your chart the hit parade
Walk in the sun don't hide in the shade
Hold your head high stand tall and proud
The softer your drum the louder your call
Do not pound it with fists of temper or greed
Nourish it gently give it time to feed
Take walks with nature sit in the sun
Open your heart to your very own drum
Listen to the pounding the ringing in your ears
The throbbing of your heart the gentle flow of tears
Listen to the laughter elation caused by pain
The sadness in your heart is never felt in vain
It can drive us to great victories
Make us feel insane
Collect all our courage
Play the waiting game
But in the end what matters
What really makes us strong
Is that we danced to our own tune
We did not just drift along

THE MEANING OF FOREVER

Forever is a word it's said
That means it goes on without end
But like forever I am told
The years go on like rays of gold
That come to us on a sunny day
And with our features like to play
For they do not die but fade away
To come again another day
Now we are like these rays of gold
We fade away when we get old
To rise again on another plane
Plan the way we will live again
For like the rainbow in the sky
It just fades out it cannot die
You my friends must realise
That like the rainbow
You cannot die

ARGUMENTS

Why do we have to argue?
To stand so straight and tall
If we could only bend
Let ourselves sometimes be small
If we could teach our ego
To turn the other cheek
In some heated moments
If we could only be mild and meek
Do we have to suffer?
Because of foolish pride
When life could be such fun
If we just flowed along with the tide
If we did not turn each ripple
Into a raging storm
For what does it really matter?
Who has the final say
If we are true to ourselves
In every other way
Let us try to remember
Next time we face a storm
Of rising mixed emotions
That can leave us so forlorn
That no one is a winner
With words said in a rage
When we are blinded by the fury
When the ego has centre stage

Let us call up to our maker
Seek our higher self
Be guided by their wisdom
Put our ego back on the shelf

HOPE

Children give us hope
They give us a brand-new day
For they are so much wiser
In oh so many ways
They fill our hearts with sunshine
They open our eyes to joy
For they help us to see beauty
In the simple things in life
To stop and smell the roses
Instead of just rushing by
Their hearts are so full of love
For each and everyone
For the fear and greed
Has not yet been set upon
The heads of these little children
So, let us try to remember
Each day we come across
One of these special children
Who are a gift from God
Not to contaminate
Lay our fears upon
Just try to surrender
Listen to their song
If we really listen
To the words they have to say
They will help us to understand
Where we went astray
Help us to recover

Some of our eternal youth
To except the life, we are given
To know the path, we have to take
To fill our lives with love
Instead of living with hate

MARRIAGE VOWS

I felt such emotion deep in my heart
My mind was spinning how did this start
There is no turning back now I can't bear to part
I have found my life partner a treasure a jewel
If I walked away now, I would be a fool
For love that is genuine is precious and rare
I will treat this heart gently with such tender care
Nourish it daily feed it with words
Of love and devotion and mean every word
We will grow together discover anew
What true love can really do
If we are open and honest loving and true
There is no limit to what we can do
So, take my hand firmly with trust in your heart
Knowing that we will never part
Gaze into my eyes see my Soul shining through
When I say the words
I do, I do

DO I CARE

Do I care for the one that hurts me so
Do I care for this one, I really don't know
Why do I weep, why do I frown
When I really should be acting the clown
For life is to short to shed so many tears
When all I need to do is face my fears
Face the fear of living alone
With nobody I can call my own
Go back to basics start from scratch
Look at what you've got and face the facts
How long can you go on this way
Pretending every things' okay
Look at the future, forget the past
Leave the hurt behind at last
Be your own person, be your own boss
Do not look back and count the cost
For material things are of little gain
When you compare them to the pain
What of life if your alone
It is not a disease it is a mile stone
A turning point a place in time
Where you must really know your mind
Learn to love and to approve
Of this person who is really you
That you have been hiding deep inside
All the while you have been wearing a disguise
Trying to walk in someone else's shoes
Who does not take the same size as you

LESSONS

The sun beats down on the concrete strip
Beats down on the golden sand
It feels hot enough to melt the Earth
To melt every grain of sand
Then a cool breeze touches my skin
Plays gently with my hair
It is times like this I understand
There is a God who cares
For every time we begin to feel
That we can take no more
He reaches out with gentle hands
To show us he is there
To show us that he understands
What we are going through
When the lessons that we set for ourselves
Seem so hard to survive
He would like to come to our rescue
To say now that is enough
But he knows that we must stumble
To learn when the going gets tough
For if he was to rescue us
Each time we had a fall
We would just go right on falling
Never learning at all
Is that not what we are here for?
To learn to stand straight and tall
To know that to love one another
Is the greatest gift of all?

A SOUL UNIQUE

Do you ever sit and wonder
Do you ever sit and think
About the life you are living
About being mild and meek
For as we begin to ponder
To let the light force in
We come up with many answers
To the questions that we seek
We begin to realise that our life is unique
That we are different to others
In the way we see and think
For we all have something special
A gift for us to share
Our part of the puzzle
That just fits right somewhere
It may be in Uganda
Where we ease one troubled mind
We may have to search the Earth
Until the day we find
The answer to our quest
That will give us peace of mind
For when our quest is over
And all the puzzle pieces fit
We will know now in our heart
That we have done our bit
That we have eased a burden
Stilled a troubled mind
Helped to find a path

That has been lost for quite some time
Opened up a doorway
So that others could pass through
Your gift may seem quite trivial
Insignificant and small
Yet to the one that who has received it
It was the greatest gift of all

NEW WORLDS A PLENTY

I seek the treetops I seek the stars
I seek the planets Neptune and Mars
I seek to rediscover what I once knew
To recall afresh with vigour and drive
To open up to come alive
To bath in the beauty
This knowledge will bring
For once the truth is free at last
I will be as one
With the Sun Moon and Stars
The Universe the Milky Way
The Galaxies the Endless Days
The New Worlds a plenty
Revealed one by one
The list is endless
If we only knew
As we are part of them
They are part of us too

WHAT DOES IT MATTER

Let us write of love at this special time
Write of love leave the pain behind
Forget the sorrow despair of the past
Live for the moment now at last
Concentrate focus the mind
On what we are doing at this point in time
What, does it matter the future the past
None of them will really last
The moment is the only thing
That we can put our faith our trust in

TRANQUILLITY

Tranquillity is the thing to seek
To ease a troubled mind
A special place where you can go
Leave all your worries behind
Loose yourself in the here and now
For just a little while
You do not need to travel
To some secluded place
All you really need to do
Is loose yourself in space
Allow your mind to wander
For just a little time
Then gently bring it back
To where you want to be this time
You may immerse yourself in the ocean
Walk along a beach
Go soaring with the eagles
Until you reach your highest peak
There are no limitations
Only those you create for yourself
Take some time to travel
Explore the inner you
The only thing to fear
Is, you and only you

WINGS OF FREEDOM

We really need to learn
To take time out for ourselves
Ease the many burdens
We sometimes create for ourselves
We need to separate ourselves
From the things that hem us in
To feel the wings of freedom
The breeze upon our skin
We need to loosen up
To learn once more to smile
To lose ourselves in laughter
For just a little while
To regain our inner strength
We need to walk some miles
For although we think they are separate
Our body mind and soul
They really are one unit
One giant energy flow
As we feed the body
We need to feed the soul
With things that make us healthy
To keep us all aglow

For there must be a balance
Between body mind and soul
If we are to find the answers
The road that we must take
A healthy mind and body
Put the soul in a state of grace

THE WRITING ON THE WALL

The trouble we are facing
In all parts of the world
Are really just the beginning
Of what we have in store
For as Mother Earth grows weaker
As her strength is sapped away
She can no longer protect us
The price we will have to pay
For all the years of terror
Of greed and neglect
We have inflicted on our Mother
Who was once so perfect
She has tried to give us warnings
To make us stop and think
About the actions we are taking
How we are making her so weak
We are continually destroying
Giving her no time to recoup
We have stripped away her protection
Torn down her lungs
Ripped apart her beauty
Exposed her to the sun
We have taken all her organs
She is dependent on
Her heart it is still beating
Though her body bleeds

For what we have not taken
We have poisoned and destroyed
The beauty that she gave us
Is now a festering sore
Yet still we keep on taking
Sowing poisons in the air
Oil spills in our oceans
Sewage from our drains
All for the mighty dollar
Is everyone insane
Can we not see the ending
The writing on the wall
Spelt out very plainly
To be seen by one and all

THE POWER OF THOUGHT

I sit and try to open my mind
Sieve through all the muddle
Sort through the layers one by one
Who knows, what I will discover
I find it hard to concentrate
I want to break away
Bury my head once more in the sand
Of false security
Where I feel safe on familiar ground
My ego is at ease
I need to find the courage
To penetrate the inner veil
Let go of old beliefs
So new ones start to flow
Materialise before my eyes
Just like a golden key
Opening doors to new frontiers
Where I at last can be freed
Freed from doubt disbelief fear
The unknown and the forbidden
I feel the weight begin to lift
My soul begins to soar
As each new truth is revealed to me
I open another door
As new knowledge penetrates
Old walls start to crumble
Walls that were built on shifting sand
Built so long ago

To block out all the light
So that the truth could not overflow
It started with just a trickle
The result of the shifting sand
The rising of my vibrations
Guided by gentle hands
With each little trickle
The light flooded in
Expanding all my knowledge
Encouraging me to look within
The shifting sands are really our thoughts
Our emotions ebbing and flowing
Building up a wall of beliefs
Without us even knowing
The power of thought
Is a mighty tool
That we use at random
To build or destroy
Play with as a toy
Gladden the heart or sadden
We could build a glorious world
If a chart we only plotted
Fill our mind with a higher kind
Of thought so long forgotten
No man is an island
Our thoughts are intertwined
Giving power to the people
One giant mind intertwined
Following a chartered course
Filled with love unconditional love
The healing guiding force
Building in strength
With each new wave
Of thought that is encountered

The energy field that is now revealed
Could move the highest mountain
Heal the sick cleanse the Earth
Reverse the greatest famine
An impossible dream
It may seem
One that could never happen
It is waiting there
For man to share
A tool he has long forgotten

Printed in the United States
By Bookmasters